PENIEL

Saint Julian Press

Poetry

Praise for *PENIEL*

"The soul in paraphrase, heart in pilgrimage, / . . . Engine against th' Almighty," George Herbert might have said of these poems, for surely he would have been as astonished and moved as I was by their intensity and range and daring. Who knew an inner life could be this rich? Imagine that God came to you once at night--"It was otherwise at first. There was the body that came / by the risen moon and again before morning," and then imagine him unaccountably turning away and growing distant and deaf. These are the cries that would pour from that wound if we had David Hopes' remarkable gifts: songs of rage and desire, songs of remembrance and lament, songs begging and bargaining and growing still, above all songs of love--"love abundant, / love unspent, untarnished, rising wave-like / till the sea is drowned." *PENIEL* is a modern daybook of Psalms, with all of their broken, hurt-into-vision grandeur. It is also, and at the same time, a work of great calmness and craft--it is, one would say, turning to Herbert again to find words to describe its hold on the reader, "something understood."

Thomas Gardner, Professor of English, Virginia Tech
John in the Company of Poets: The Gospel in Literary Imagination

"David Brendan Hopes consecrates his book as a site of revelatory power, inviting his readers to join him in wrestling with the hardest questions of human existence — the problems of suffering and evil, the mysteries of beauty and grace. Hopes sings of these things with a prophetic honesty and clarity of vision, and so the mercy he finds is hard–learned and all the more profound. Throughout *PENIEL* readers will catch glimpses of the face of God."

Evan Gurney – Assistant Professor of English
at University of North Carolina Asheville

PENIEL

Poems

by

David Brendan Hopes

SAINT JULIAN PRESS
HOUSTON

Published by
SAINT JULIAN PRESS, Inc.
2053 Cortlandt, Suite 200
Houston, Texas 77008

www.saintjulianpress.com

ISBN-13: 978-0-9986404-5-7
ISBN: 0-9986404-5-X
Library of Congress Control Number: 2017956189

Cover Art & Design
Tâché Impressionism ~ Ron Starbuck
Jacob Wrestling with the Angel
1865 by Alexander-Louis Leloir

Author Photo Credit: William Zane Lawrence
From a Performance of Shakespeare's ~ *As You Like It*

PREFACE

So Jacob was left alone, and a man wrestled with him till daybreak. When the man saw that he could not overpower him, he touched the socket of Jacob's hip so that his hip was wrenched as he wrestled with the man. Then the man said, "Let me go, for it is daybreak."

But Jacob replied, "I will not let you go unless you bless me."

GENESIS 32:24–26 (NIV)

"He who approaches near to me one span, I will come near to him one cubit; and he who approaches near to me one cubit, I will approach near to him one fathom; and whoever approaches me walking, I will come to him running; and he who meets me with sins equivalent to the whole world, I will greet him with forgiveness equal to it."

MISHKAT-UL-MASABIH

"Shall not God be put to the test? It is my one duty on this earth."

THIS BOOK IS DEDICATED TO THE MEMORY OF
DICK FALKENSTEIN AND NEIL ZABRISKIE

C O N T E N T S

PENIEL

EVERY ANGEL IS TERROR.

AND SO I HOLD MYSELF BACK AND SWALLOW THE CRY
OF A DARKENED SOBBING. AH, WHO THEN CAN
WE MAKE USE OF? NOT ANGELS: NOT MEN,
AND THE RESOURCEFUL CREATURES SEE CLEARLY
THAT WE ARE NOT REALLY AT HOME
IN THE INTERPRETED WORLD.

RAINER MARIA RILKE
DUINO ELEGIES
THE FIRST ELEGY

TRANSLATE BY A.S. KLINE © 2001

CHRISTMAS MORNING

The bare ground shows its bones,
the curved, hard down, the female hills,
the creeks raw as new cuts in the valleys.
Rain for Christmas. I go walking.
Gray, the land, like a whale's back
studded with spears, the bare trees.
Dry, the honey of deceit in the lily's throat,
honey of generation in the strangle-vine;
rose dead in her intricacies.
Arrayed on the forest floor are Christmas fern,
partridge berry, Eve-color still, enduring green.
Birdless, this silence.
They have twittered off to Bethlehem.
Christmas morning the village bells
toll me as I walk.
Who's there? ask the bareness,
    the bright Eve berries.
I answer, "A poet, Christmas morning."
Ease, they whisper, *let the line.*
    Give us slack.

ADVENT SEQUENCE

1

Some choose the lights of the malls,
the thronged marquees of multiplexes,
People of the Right Hand, and that hand full.
Some-- I tell you from the most intimate authority--
creep from the sidewalks, declining
into ways made crooked by the fear of onlookers.

Yes, I have been talking to the Men of God again.
They are interesting to me because
able to find condemnatory verses apt
to everything I love. Willingly for them I perfume myself
with cologne of sulphur. Willingly I put on diamond
shoes so as to tread the brimstone deeper in.
But wholly without flippancy, you understand,

believing the Paradise they cross their swords before,
cherishing and desiring every particle which
must be left behind. You know the rules.
All would be hollow without some sacrifice.
And let us not imagine greater drama than obtains:
a man who has failed at everything departs

the theater of his loss and goes-- does he care where?
so long as it is deeper, hotter, a blunter god's
blast furnace where something must at last
-- out of compact and furious energy-- come to pass.
I do not know what works for other men.
I have gone to war again.

2

Howling again at dawn's brink, that scent of
cinnamon and alcohol and sweat I came to measure
the glories of the night with--
I too see little to be gained. Yet,
to put on beauty of the Beast's pelt, ambrosial
and imperiled, to lie down in the red rose and
wake in the white .
Where? Anywhere. Oh, but one must *go*.

    (Some men think a flower is enough.
     There is no flower.
     There are turtlehead and orchis.
     There is the right,
      the invisible heart's double.)

3

We are old, declares the very sun at waking.
I answer that each inch forward from this white meridian
requires some novel violence, a wilder civility.
Sun reads from the Book of Entropies
where his own name comes-- and mine--
in violet of a hesitating flame.

For a bitter hour I become all lovers slamming doors
on all their lovers, the loved one crooning
in a pool of blood and silk, bewildered.
I wrench my soul into a rifle cocked
against heaven, heart a bullet
in a purple chamber, not then God's or anybody's love.

I am changed: Fury etched in diamonds on an iron collar.
I shift in the darkness but do not answer.
We are old now sun says sanely
climbing Beaucatcher in a spray of pines.
Against him I offer this dark courtesy,
this morning of defiance, this brute twist eastward.

4

Like a minor god in an epic-- absurd but memorable--
I come howling prophesies of our future, bearing
our history before me like bronze armor
useless equally for affront or defense,
the prop of an old heroic play
to which the script is lost, ungainly,

vulnerable to the tongue's most casual artillery.
This is not the prudent way.
I don't claim this hoarse cry from the crags
is appropriate,
merely what I know.
Merely what remains of a riot of attempts.

It could last forever, our warfare drawn like music
from the next apartment, incessant, overheard--
or like gold wire in a poem, fine as a boy's hair,
an expensive conceit, unspendable-- our
lies innocent because never uttered so as to be believed.
If only you were not so beautiful.

If only the silver slackened from your voice
one could shift one's longing to the ordinary world,
its exhausted faces in the light,
exhausted murmurs in the dark.
But wave by wave the sweetness enters. By dawn I have
forgotten that I meant to win.

Take off your veils and I decide what to believe.
At your bones' cunning the guarded town
unhinges gates, throws down its stones to sing.
Skin of your flanks is the gold fruit Eve's teeth marred.
Beauty whirls upon you, squandered, hourly reborn.
I dip my garments in the blazing water.

5

I'm trying to identify what in the garden has such perfume,
this wedding of lilac and orange,
a feast of stone fruit with dancers and burning torches after.

Not rose.
Not trampled mint.
I thought of those.

Perhaps this:
I remember the hour when I wept into the snow,
letting tears fall as they might.
A melodramatic gesture unless something came of it,
which I think now was the sowing,
by one inconsolable,
of consolation, of love by one whom love
had passed:
tear flowers, if you like,
bells-of-sorrow, blue when not invisible,
exuding such confounding fragrance on the air.

It is your doing.
Accept the blame this time.
Lilac and orange,
stone fruit juiced
and licked from the chests.
of dancers,
the burning torches after.

6

Oh now, Blank and Overarching Dark,
I will teach you how to love me.
It is not ease forth nor falling.
It is a word spoken in bitterness
against bitterness.
It is time speaking against eternity.
If it were easy someone would have said.
The crack of fist on tooth, the cleanser,
faceless rivals censed by beer and blood
and time jerked back by fistfuls of bright hair.
I will tell you how to love me.
Lightning woos the mountain. Like that.
Hawk and sparrow. Pool under root.
Force and sacrament and secret strength.
Do not whisper of the soul tonight.

I see us in the deeds of beasts,
quick to flight, fear a red moon
betraying our way among the trees.
Broom-legged birds, the pelicans
a-haunt above the water on Cretaceous wings.
I catch our terror in the speeding headlights.
I feel us shrink from screams of steel,
from forests shattered, animals escaping
without comprehension and without farewell.
Fear like an arched flame blinds the stars.
Loathing without hope or history.
Yet in moments of imperfect hatred,
circling back, resisting and abiding,
 by night returning to the broken nest,
 holding our ground till day.

7

Love is leather and sweat in a sealed room.
It rips the gold ring from its ear
to cleanse the night with scarlet.
It coos down deities and takes
their tongues into its throat.
 It peels off flesh longing to be bare enough.

Love follows ram-cocked boys,
spreadeagles on the backstreet,
moaning amid boots and glass.
Love leaks blood into the sheets by morning.
Love by the hungry moon goes out,
 unsatisfied, passes your window without looking.

8

I won't stand here always
sore as one tree in a plowed field.
I will speak, but speak of
the brittle stem, hard knot of the rose,
the bitten, imperfect garden.

I will talk of the dark
at the hollow of your throat.
I will say you are a marsh bird
flushed by night, when the lamp is out
and there's no way of telling.

I will say, "There's a tree
upon the mountain" and expect
you alone will know my meaning.
I will say,
"There is a pool against a wall of ice."

9

Ferret comes to nibble from my hand.
Thrush takes its small food.
In dreams I am sustained by compassionate wild eyes.
In dreams the animals aid me
for my animal
as God shall never aid me for my god.

In dreams love takes the shapes of animals.
Soul tries pinion, carapace, fang.
Each beast is love's deed done in bone:
she-hawk, starved, urgent beyond wind;
jackal and viper, boar-bear roaring in briar,
scold-squirrel, weaving spider,

pike ambusher in the water,
she-wren ragging the fringes with her rage,
hurt lion hungering; satyr broken under stone;
skulkers and stalkers in the shadow,
poised to strike, to run;
rattler coiled about the feet;

images of love slant and set aside,
visions of postponement, cruelty, and squalor,
love defeated, stillborn, crying under weights;
doe swift to flight; buck on the black crag bellowing,
dogs yap, sniff, rut in bitch heat
waiting till love wolfs them;

cats ripped from their fur,
wing-shield raised, fang bared against the Adversary;
weasel wrought to wolverine,
plodder become swallow, brute butterflyed,
the hideous shed skin by skin,
failed love up rung by rung toward the waiting Lover.

On signal the sleepers and the dead
gather their frost pelts and run.
Slatted barn floors flow with honey.
Crow flaps against the gold wave.
Wolverine at edge of tundra lopes,
spine arched, teeth bared to the arising.

Bear stirs from a dream of mauling.
Ibex kicks laurel of snow to the glory,
to that diamond of first water,
the fireball rolling night away.
Gryphon, Centaur, Basilisk--
longing splits the beast skin;

claws turn to hand-palm, raised.
And when they are men and women,
they find who must forgive,
walk with them outward hand in hand,
stilled with hush of homing,
upon a path too bright to see.

10

Blessed be rat that skitters in the night,
    be owl that breaks the rat's back,
the bloody weasel gnawing owls' bones.
    Blessed be the voice I heard in blackness,
the invisible lamenter,
    howling the secrets of the heart.
Blessed be this gut sickness,
    body's vomit, mind's ejection
older than song, cleansing the song.
    Blessed the six seeds that bound
Our Lady to hell. Blessed the warfare
    to get out and over.
Blessed the face at the window I forget,
    my first face scoured and gone.
Blessed the cat's paw,
    the power in the shell's lime,
the crab's vise,
    force in the veins of stone,
brain, fur, viscera,
    in incomprehensible fire,
the Axe, the Annihilator--
    Blessed the way out.
Blessed Arcturus torching the mountain.
    The hunter's cry in sorrow of the hunt.

Blessed, O blessed that this night dies.

11

When the wolf moon howls, when the juncos,
migrants to this bitter land,
twitter their testament of somewhere worse;
when the creek is stiffened silver and
her sleepers, the frogs and chrysalides,
breathe crystal into crystal space;

when creatures caught in the open weave their last dream
with the dream of dead planets, colder, brighter,
never again to wake: Lord, I think of You.
Stars sag on Pisgah. Moon closes to the ridge,
gun-metal silver rolling on the mountain,
bright rim to black rim, a crushing wheel

gouged by the December of the trees.
Moon's flak bursts against the owl's wings.
Blaze and black contend.
I kneel on stone. I gather from Hominy Creek the blue
glaze shining and shifted, the finger-freezing mercury.
I gather the lights. I hoard the weapons to my hand—-

pity, fury, a human face ringed with its
inevitable nimbus of tears.
After long silence I have returned--
"For You" it is best to say, but we know better.
All in ambush, God, against Thee.
I lurk in night and make my poem.

       Go, song, I tell it.
    Go to the owl cross-winged over Pisgah.
      Go to the coon hound-bayed, to spider weaving
         in her broil of hunger.
    Go, song. Tell how heart succeeds from wound to flame.
     Tell who holds his little blasphemies into the wind.
       Go tell them.
  Say I lift my fist to the judging stars.
    Say if they threaten I eat their hearts.
      Say if they circle I meet them whirling.
  Say if they condemn I vomit wind and fire.
    Say whatever thing they maim, I parry healing equal.

Go song to my lovers lost by knife and plague
and sadness in the dark that named them blameless
forward from their birthday Edens.

Oh, unaccountably by night
I start to sing. See how the beauties float
from the ground with their dead rose laurels to listen.
See them lean in,
shaking their gold heads, twangling their lutes
with single strings, hearing no cry from me
not cried already
by children lost in the dark woods of the world
before the worlds began.
Child, they say, *child*.

Like owls in gray roosts they natter
how all had ground to silence all the same before.
But I ask a gift of them one by one.
They listen. Sigh. They pull something
from their vault of bones. I accept.
It is their hearts. I eat.

Go song.
Say I lift hands to the One who I remembrance.
Say if He comes walking I will greet Him running.
Say if He carries a candle I come wreathed in fire.
Say if He comes in wrath I come the panther on the white hill.
Say if he comes singing, my throat is the phoenix on the gold tree
Say if He repent, I answer forgiveness equal to the world.

HYMN TO THE BLESSED VIRGIN MARY FOR THE SOUL OF ALFONSO X, KING OF CASTILE

In the tales it goes that from the mouth
of one who sang for you entwines at death
a bush with five red roses.
In each rose five bees hum *Maria,*
five notes, a harmony hung for paradise
while the world turns elsewhere winter.

Pilgrims of this road wake weeping.
Each tear is evidence of violent country:
the shot stag bleeding among the lilacs,
the white thrush wounded in the rosebush
fashion song with not a false comparison
and no rhyme strained.

I sing no more for other women, but to regain
through you all things lost in them.
I arrive out of nowhere,
offering one stark white lily,
singing against girls with feathers
in their hearts, against a cartwheel star

wrecking the sleep of shepherds in the hills.
Let your eyes like eyes of roses
blossom from your tears.
The rude wood's rotted away.
Where it stood the blood thorn flowers and flowers.
Its petals sear the hem of frost.

Hard lovers hide their hearts like jewels in boxes.
Men who capered in their jewels and furs
have won you, Lady; what's their need?
Out of your rosebud turret, Lady, overflow.
Set bow to the strings. Shake thy gown of many colors.
I too stand naked in the snow. Must dance.

THE ANNUNCIATION
Jan van Eyck

In this Northern Annunciation
do not anticipate conflict
between conviction and observation.
To be thought of is to be achieved.
The rainbow hilarious archangel
warps the floor with real weight.
The Holy Ghost descends like
a circus dancer on a golden wire,
smaller than doves in life,
as if to affirm the miracle
survives the carnival of externals.
Mary says her lines upside-down
for His convenience.
The agent of a bashful love,
the angel brings her lilies,
smiling sweetly at it all,
ear cocked to the tramp
of kingdoms in the lily's throat.
The Testament, an afterthought
cut in an incidental floor,
holds this jewel, this sky-larking up.

THE MEETING OF ST. ANTHONY AND ST. PAUL
Sassetta

It is a sort of paradise,
an Eden of obsession
in which each attainment
longs again, and harder,
until the soul eats up
the miles, the barriers,
this intolerable creation.

And here stand two beautiful old men
with rings of light about their heads,
crooked, we would think,
or aligned with some unsuspected center.
Earth lies squared by golden sky,
by the harmonious, unlikely trees.
Road runs like a reading eye
from west high to east low, stone-strewn,
haunted by demons from the druid wood.
Here is the centaur
who longs to graze among the angels.
Before the cave, upon the stones
of the greenish road, is the fulcrum.
For here Paul has gone a step
up Anthony's way,
Anthony a step down Paul's.
Here the flower halos sink their roots.

GEORGES DE LA TOUR: *THE PENITENT MAGDALEN*
circa 1640

Folded to mark a page never returned to,
you find a picture of yourself
    walking among sunflowers.
A blue cap tilts back on your head,
leaving room on your brow for a slash of light
brash enough to throw the balance off,
a wayward brightness capturing the eye
    which for an instant holds all wisdom.
You remember the moment, the happiness
you thought would never fade
    yet which, as it turned out, never came again.
You recall the sunburst of the flowers
at your chest like lovers listening for the rhythm
    of the hearts of lovers,
the white rose beating in the iron cage.
    You hold the photograph so shadow falls
upon the face, that one time beautiful,
difficult now to look upon. Whose was it really?
Was it your face before the present world?

    Say to one who happens by,
as though some apology were in order,
"Who was I to walk among sunflowers like a man?"

You take the brush and paint--
not quite frantically, not quite without purpose,
though to an onlooker
    somewhat beyond the necessary passion.
You paint a kestrel hovering midair,
wings bent like a dove's,
with bloodier and more beautiful intent.

    You paint the legend of a lover
who burst into flame
when his lady, laughing, slammed the door.
Compassion guides the clenched lines,
the shell-curve modeling of the hand

lifted to the mouth in horror.
You paint how he burned for seven hours,
standing straight up, arms outstretched,
Jove-bolted tree of two sad branches
        shivered suddenly to scarlet flower.
How she, fleeing into farther rooms,
still saw the flicker on the wall,
        still his green eyes unconsumed
amid the leaping gold, through any curtain,
through clenched hands and wet lids of her eyes.

On a day of no particular distinction,
        and she no longer young.

Wait for the critics to sift through flames
        to the ash of stately consummation.
        They will praise details:
The miniature on the lady's wall,
in which the princess
falls among the dragons.
In the painting's window, clear and small,
a mantis snags a blown leaf with her
saw-tooth arms, bites the pointless gold,
swiveling her green head toward starvation.

        Use what you have.
                Of the rest, assume the worst.

As in De La Tour's *The Penitent Magdalen*, less obvious
effects make epics in a little:
the bracelets orphaned in the shadow at her feet,
the rope of pearl whose paleness

        balances the paleness of a skull.
The pearl has changed its metaphor
from frippery to a Kingdom,
nature unspecified but of great price.
        A woman gazes through a mirror
at the black behind the mirror.

A woman in a red dress in the great darkness
of the world. One candle.

    The zig-zag of the red dress
is a stairway-- steep, broken--
she has mounted half way up.
    Genius here is to reveal
nothing in the mirror, nothing that she sees
but flame in flesh tone, leaping.
The flame burns opposite the heart
    in the saint's uncovered breast:
a juxtaposition, as if accidental,
of the candle like a full moon
burning sweat and perfume from the tousled room.
It is the exterior image of a heart.
    In flame-tone it roars up.
Or is poised to roar in this instant
of final, agonized repose.

Before that instant when you realize there is no mirror
but your own eyes into which the saint's eyes
terribly descend.

    Saint Mary Red Dress!
you might cry into the quiet,
thinking should she turn to see her torment
in the gilt black crystal of your face,
should she mate her heart with your heart,
    you might catch flame,
      comet-like take flight on red pinions
      that are the lead weights of your passions

      all transformed,
lift on them finally,
unquenchable, larking
in a cloud of squandered ointment
    out these penitential rooms and over.

ON THE ADORATION OF THE SHEPHERDS

God is born tonight in the next town.
Be serious. Who wouldn't go?
Lock the back door. Turn the furnace down.
Throw a handful of food at the dog. Blow
off the dinner with the couple you really like.
Riffle through the bills for those
which absolutely will not wait. Take a hike.
The way? The consequence? The point? Who knows?
Select a path, an avenue, goat trail, a turnpike,
on through the twilight and the early snows.
Angel voices are, of course, a plus,
but go in dark and silence if you must.
Remember to seek the narrowest wretched door.
Prepare to diminish, resign, dispense, adore.

GAZELLE DRINKING FROM ONE OF THE RIVERS OF PARADISE

Two figures are cut in white stone,
an animal, a stylized spray of water.
Byzantine, all curve and counter-curve,
arc set against scallop,
vertical curved space at rest;
horizontal curved space flowing, flowing.
It told some holy story once, the point
forgotten but for this square of broken frieze.
It is a gazelle drinking from a river of Paradise.

From the gazelle's posture we know
it is in that Paradise which comes after Eden.
The gazelle has not lost the habit
of standing with its hind hooves poised to spring.
Its reflex for flight is a gesture of humility.
Nothing can harm it here. But it has come
a long way to drink from this river,
and does not suppose that fleet limb,
wise nose brought it all the way.

It says what saves us is a gift, always.
To smell lost home behind and not turn back.
To pick a route between two sheets of snow
and see a first thaw turn the mud to dazzle.
To hear, to wake and know the tune
is the ancient river running inexhaustible.
To walk on its banks and drink the water,
immaculate, cool, worth waiting for
even had you no thirst left.

The gazelle is perceived not as it is
but according to the place one looks from.
To those who are not yet home in Paradise,
its countenance will seem
ceremonial, hieratic, utterly at peace.
It drinks forever like a figure in white stone,
drinking, river running, until a world is filled.
Those who are home will see it
drink, leap up, and praise.

LINES TO BE SET BY WILLIAM BYRD

The animals dead at the roadside
bore messages, I think, though it's hard
to tell with their countenances
transmogrified like that.

Baby raccoon, paying out pink gut
over its shoulder witnesses for what
small thing it's ended at the start:
an elder crossed, a big dog's gesture

misinterpreted. The crows
assign themselves to pick at it
until the eyes with their accusations
are dug out.

You'd think a bird alert enough
to get away. What kind was it?
One reddish feather waves "surrender"
in a language the 3 bus could not read.

The Christmas puppy with its rib cage shattered
kept life enough to crawl into a ditch
where its mistress wouldn't find it
till there was no recognizing anymore.

Good, you say, to one mercy
in the midst of holocaust,
to one horror left in obscurity
amid the thousand roadsides.

The opossum really was too stupid to have
lived so long. This story was mine. I caught
her in the headlights some hour after midnight,
trotting side to side,

pointing her grin of terror, her ruby eye
backwards to see what was about to murder her.
I stopped a dead stop, face in the steering wheel.
It took that much. Waited

for her to find at last her stupid way.
Sion is wasted. Refugees glide like ghosts
across the seven rivers. Children
drink from the poison pools.

Sion deserta facto est. It is late.
The sanitation trucks are busy. You could
shovel them off the road yourself,
but for the fear some witness would be lost.

RECTIFICATION OF THE ANGLES OF ASCENT

Nothing rises as you think it will.
Not the standing water hurled airborne
        by the delivery truck,
not the jay startled to his blue diagonal,
not the petals of the crape myrtle
        unexpectedly rising
as if tutored by their gang of bees.
The mountains at the bottom of the world
        go the wrong way altogether.

The power that calls *down* calls from the center
and moves when the center moves.
        You should not look for that.
The power that calls *up* is more diffuse,
summoning *here* and *here*
        from where it wasn't half an hour ago.
The implication? Ascent is available
whatever direction you hope to be traveling.
        It accepts the beetle and the peacock
and certain people hurrying sideways
and lets that count as "up."
        "Up" is egalitarian, you might say, or
lonesome for a lover, lost,
who might return from anywhere.

        (The extended lines of the pyramids
make other pyramids in the air.
You'd think people who go on about
        such things
would have noted this. Only Nekhbet, finally,
wings outspread above her deserts,
        fulfils expectations, by virtue of eternity)

The rectification of the angles of ascent
requires the parting of the seas to reveal
            the paths those souls will take
on the last day, rising up
from his embrace, regretful at first
            into the unfamiliar light. Laid bare
must be the hidden palaces and passageways,
the routes the gods have taken in secret
            while our attention was elsewhere.
At some point after comes
the realignment of all ascending things,
            that what was the destination from the first
might be, at last, descried, wings tilted,
feathers trimmed for the first, and final, certain flight.

ZEAL FOR THY HOUSE

Zeal for Thy House, Lord,
        has made me a beggar, at evening
        gazing into the windows of those
        gathered around the table.
        Some eat. I do not.
        Thy name was honey on my tongue.

Zeal for Thy House, Lord,
        has made me a wanderer.
        After a glimpse inside Thy mansions,
        what other house would hold me?
        I went naked to the bridal chamber.
        The door was locked against me.

Zeal for Thy House, Lord,
        has made me a burglar.
        Blooms a red rose in the neighbor's garden
        and the wall is high.
        There are thorns for one who falls,
        and one must fall.

Zeal for Thy House, Lord,
        has changed my voice
        from the voice of a man
        into what I cannot say—
        half swan, half lamentation;
        half silence, half settling snow.

Zeal for thy house, Lord
        has left me with one song
        and none who listen.

PENIEL

This winged thing, this spirit
with the hard hands—

whichever way I turn it stops me.
I would go forward. I would be stopped.

That I should be a god enfolded by the wings of god
was not told me in my infancy.

I was not prepared. I turn to the east and to the west.
I have a red stone for pillow.

That deep I could not pierce
but fold around me like a blanket

That feast not to be considered yes or no
but to be lapped like honey

That food which is a body,
and the eating is a further hunger

That dark not evil nor ignorance
but the covering veil

And the light which walks before him where he walks
and the light which walks before me where I walk

(Who is turbulence and who is peace
can never now be known)

That the body of light come forth
from the body of fire

flame from the shadow of flame,
light from the calamities of light

from the breath of wrestlers,
from the murmuring of bones

from the pits of corruption
this one pure thing.

Before thee fled I from my own voice.
Before thee I was nothing.

(Peniel is this place, where we wrestle until daybreak.
I will not let you go even should you bless me.)

AVE DONNA SANTISSIMA

Women are singing in the twilight.
Three, I think. There could be more.

Maiden most married they sing,
Level pathway. Golden door.

Lucky in missteps
three times three

Women are singing behind a wall
where I cannot see

Scarlet and argent
Purple and pall.

A garden enclosed, I think.
The bower. The Eden hidden.

Touch unlooked-for
Kiss unbidden.

I know of men who prayed
bitterly to a bitter tree,

who woke then, crying,
No more for others. All for thee.

Women are singing in the darkness,
neither wearied nor flagging in invention:

discord, harmony, two voices one,
one voice three: a trembling suspension.

I've heard the fateful spindles spun,
have heard the tolling of the golden hour.

A girl is opening an iron door
A girl is stooping for a snowy flower.

The avenging wind
that trounced the town

kissed you
when it blew the steeples down.

Bow set to the strings,
lips set to the reed.

Play only to those
who come in need.

Out of the dusty yellow clay
out of the shavings of the day

Out of the midden
out of the molder

sculpt him anew.
Make him strong. Make him kind.

Wings at the shoulder
Gold preceding. Golden behind

Take you my eyes.
Take you my mind.

THE SOUL'S CAPACITY TO BEAR SADNESS

I have been exploring the soul's capacity to bear sadness.

To do this I have summoned the image of my mother
in her white nightgown, bent over,
crying in the midnight hallway, I forget why.

I have thought of my little black and white dog
who died when I was away at school,
but who came to me in a dream, and it was perfect,
and all the long-loved voices drifted out the windows,
and it was a night of blessing, of forgiveness--
then behind came the strange, dark waters
with their other voices, alluring and unfamiliar.
I tried to enter.
They tell me not to dwell on that.

Oh, be transparent, the midnight voices said,
leave nothing obscure. Leave nothing behind.

I thought of my knuckles reddening your door,
you on the other side listening, curious,
as though more than one thing might have happened.

I think of my poems with their goods on their backs
like refugees shambling through an unanticipated wasteland.

I think of laugher behind a closing gate.
Go ahead, one says to the heart. *Get it all out.*
This is our experiment. This is what we need to know.

It's a study which does not repay too much concentration.
Looking from somewhere to the side is best.
Left field. Through an album of somebody else's lovers.
A touch here, a rill of fragrance,
a syllable uttered so that you must break stride.

Does the world know how much can be borne
and leave the soul the soul?
Are there records to be broken?
Does it expect growth in this arena?
Does it anticipate
some bad expansion deeper down and darker in?

The goldfish you took the trouble to name
glides amid the rocks you bothered to stack just right.
He must be blessed, you think, dwelling among
the stems of waterlilies. He eats from your hand.
He could be extinguished by the tilting of a rim.
You could do it. Once thought of, it's hard
to push it from your mind.

Said some certain way, you have to laugh at annihilation.
You have to think of it as one of those
uncomplicated ironies even children understand.

The four-rayed starbursts of the foam flowers
throng between the porch slats. You remind yourself
they are for a day. One only. Do not touch. Move on.

His email says "I love you."
It means something, even if no more
the meaning that you Lionhearted for
when Jerusalem might yet be won. Those days are gone.
You love him back, of course. You say so and hit "Send."

You hear your own cry somewhere this side of the horizon.
You look out, trying to fathom how it came to be,
the softness that makes cruelty easy,
the cruelty that makes kindliness absurd.
Maybe the marsh hibiscus with its Sauron eye of wheeling fire.
The lads in the street, their bad vocabulary. Maybe that.

The radio in the next room plays something beautiful.
You are content to listen from a distance,
knowing that there is, essentially, no approach,
knowing you will not be able to refrain
from turning forever to the point
where the last of you went down.

WHO IS WALKING IN MY GARDEN

Twice I've gotten up to see who is walking in my garden.
It's not easy to get into without my seeing.
If it is you, welcome.
You finally answered the invitation I sent long ago,
     that said you could return whenever you wanted,
     no questions asked;
     that I would watch from the window,
     or run out to greet you, however you imagined it.
You do not even bend the grass.
You gather the man-high cosmos to you
     as if they were gangly children.
You whisper to them, or they whisper to you.
     I can't tell from here.
A late iris comes back to try again.
You went to it. You touched its petals.
I could withhold and withdraw for decades
     and not be so light of touch.
Can't be sure if it was you, of course,
     except by subtraction of all things evident.
I am trying to remember what you especially treasured,
     whether it was roses, and if roses,
     red or white or golden; the curve or the angle,
     the dapple or the blaze of light.
If you could leave me a note, if you could whisper
     to the hydrangeas who will whisper to me.
I will make it so before you come again.

ON THE VIGIL OF SAINT THOMAS

Over at last,
the Christmases of my childhood,
expectant, full of mercy and tenderness,
secret deeds of sweetness done so the Mystery
might come to His remembered home,
when even in sleep ears bent to the gather of wings
above the rooftops, the rainbow angels
choiring at last *here* and *now*.

Now like the rest I go grumbling through
the winter streets, hating the crowds,
the cost, the misdirection of it all.
Hating Santa and the hawking elves.
Hating Gabriel for not answering any
of the questions a girl would ask.
Hating Joseph for not calling ahead.
Hating the parties to which I am not invited.
Hating the angels for their cruel salutation,
the golden promise never to be repeated.
Hating myself for growing old.

Still, it is better than sometimes before.
I've not once this season sought an alley
to hide in from the lights and revelers,
bent double with grief against the halving of my life.

I will admit something to you, since we're friends.
I have not changed. I have gone underground.
Greedy like the rest, I offer that
the buying and selling is a memory
of celestial desire, which, too long thwarted,
turns to obtainable things.

Lord Buddha trussed in Christmas lights,
      I have not given up desire.
Child Jesus barefoot in the snowfields,
      I have not given up desire.
God the Father grisly on the white heights,
      I have not given up desire.
God the Spirit haunting Scrooge's cocoa mug,
      I have not given up desire.
Black Mother silent on the black throne,
      I have not given up desire.

It goes underground like the tunnels of the mice,
a circuit between caches of dry seed.

It was always of the spirit, my desire,
taking the bodies of flesh for the sake of poetry.
      Shame on all who were deceived.
      Shame on all who withheld
on the basis of such elementary misapprehension.

After the shame, now, you must utter a blessing.
Nothing much.
Bless what you have stolen.
Bless what withered with the wait.
Bless what I should not have done without.

THE VIGIL OF THE NATIVITY

The angels arrived and they asked me who I was
that I should see a miracle.
They said, "Are you mighty?"
and I answered, "Compared to what?"
They said, "Have you wisdom?"
and I did not know.
"Are you pure?" they said, "for only the eyes
of the pure shall see."
And I answered, "I have heard this asked before,
when Moab & Ammon & Amalek & Canaan & Egypt & Aram
       prepared their little ones for sacrifice.
I have heard this asked before when the brothers of the blood
were driven under the wheels, and the singing women were
       beaten into clay."

      And they began "Who are you--"
But I stopped them, shouting, having for the first
time known myself,
     "I am a furnace of beryl.
     I am a golden loom.
     I am the Tiger, the Outpouring. Listen.
     If I were pure I would have broken like the oaks
         that will not bend.
     If I were pure I would have loved the love of statues,
     moon struck marble sighing over moving shadows.
     If I were pure the arrows and spearheads which bring
     compassion would not know where to land.
     If I were pure I would have fled the shadow who has
         made me a man.
     If I were pure I would have died
     when the officers of the law
         bore false witness against me, when
         fingers were pointed and the laughter rang.

If I were pure I'd have fallen down and worshiped
        a spectre of the gods,
the Face of Judgment burning over its Sword.
If I were pure I would scorn the weak and withhold the secret
        from the seeker.
If I were pure I would have kindled the fire my little room,
        the little dwellings of my followers.
If I were pure Saint Mary Red Dress would not know me.
If I were pure I would have crushed the spider and the worm.
If I were pure I would be a gorgon of certainty and discord.
If I were pure I would see what you came to show,
        the forges and anvils and the diamond wheels.
If I were pure the Gate of the Midnight City would not
        slam closed, nor Purity and slavery
        vanish in one instant.
If I were pure I would not burst so into song even against
        the Angels of the Dispensation,
        nor flow like a river of many streams
        nor drop tears down into the gardens and palaces,
        cleansing and bringing to life."

    And I answered, "Who are you to ask?
    Yes, I am mighty. Tremble and fly home."

A BOOK OF CAROLS

1

Carol of the Christ Child's Garden

Come into my garden
The Christ Child said to me,
*Here is the lily for what's past,
the rose for what's to be.*

*Here is the emerald mound
where love lies till the day
all sleeping souls must rise and do
what the hardest scriptures say.*

*Here is the sapphire pool
from which the laughing river ran
all through Paradise, and by
the melancholy carnivals of man.*

*For every poison on the earth
here grows the remedy,
For every slaughtered soldier lad,
a purple-flowered tree.*

*Here I will croon your sleep awhile,
then teach you how to make
a firebrand for the morning's,
a gold bird for the evening's sake.*

2

Carol of the Infuriated Hour

The stab to the heart that is such music,
the light beyond brightness that is such sight--
For the sake of this season in the stories
I will cease my wars with God tonight.

I will choose, with open eye, the talking beasts,
the white-in-the-snowdrift Christmas rose,
the legends of wandering a bitter way,
high hill and desert, for what?— God knows.

Someone turned the rose-tree to a cross
and the angels' murmur into penitential song:
such is the ancient sorrow: they who stole
the stories have the stories wrong.

What saved the old ones in the tangled land,
amid assorted enemies, is what saves still:
to see the white stag in the tangled wood,
the Cross and the Rose on the same snow hill

We are saved in our infuriated hour--
by cunning softened, by omnipotence beguiled--
by the newborn tempest crooked upon our arm,
motherly murmuring to him, *child, my child.*

3

She the Sojourner

She the sojourner was the first
of those who sweetly came before.
Mother of David through many fathers,
Mother of Christ through many more.

Thebes was golden, Nineveh was iron,
the kings in their chariots, who thinks of them?
But I will tell you a mystery:
lily and rose from a single stem.

Lady before the Lady, chosen bride.
Who would guess that all should yield,
given time and the wheels that turn the world,
to Ruth who gleaned the yellow field.

In the pictures they shall paint
the rose and the lily at your breast,
the crown, the cross, the empty tomb,
the white bird flown the broken nest.

4

Carol of Joseph

The lights go out one by one.
The last bells of midnight ring.
Joseph sleeps murmuring *My son.*
Who preferred God to everything,
God prefers to everything.

As a father bending over,
as a mother at the cradle's side,
as some watcher watching overmuch.
We've hung the injured boughs with green.
We've hushed the ticking of the clocks.

What we would give to keep you safe tonight
is given back, boundless as a sea.
I'll hold you a little until light.
Sleep, murmur, jewel in my jewel box;
Dream of the doorway. Dream of me.

A SONG OF MERCIES

Mercy on me Spirit,
        for my excessiveness in all things,
        unrepentant, sorrowing that there
        was not always substance nor occasion for more.
        What I have touched I have worn out.
        Where I have gone has wished to
        see the back of me.
        What I have sought has been run to ground
        or soared off crying
        where none could find it anymore.
        Whom I have loved has turned from me
        finally in exhaustion--
        and I know that saying it this way
        makes it sound, almost, a virtue,
        a fire, consuming or refining, in either case white hot--
        but you decide, and permit the proper mercy to descend.

Mercy on me Spirit,
        for the fierce lucidity,
        the stuff of poetry, but the man-destroyer,
        the fender-off of hearts;
        for the charity almost never withheld
        but sometimes crammed down the wrong throat,
        a feast for the merely peckish,
        the starving left with a high smile and a poem
        prostrate in the road;
        for the ingratitude that takes Arcturus and the Pleiades
        and Bach, El Greco and the red tailed hawk as merely due;
        for the pride that would unmake the world
        to make You answer me, to
        make You yield me what is mine,
        to make You love me as you must have promised
        in that swaddling hour only I remember.

Mercy on me Spirit,
        lame with anger, song by anger struck out of my mouth,
        dancer of the Kali-dance: *revenge, revenge*;
        by anger's red moon put to sleep,
        by anger's red sun wakened,
        poems wrenched into timepieces of retribution,
        nights into counting houses of Your slights and wrongs,
        reveries and friendships shattered;
        having built a house of anger to dwell within;
        having been a river of anger plowing underground;
        having been a wind of anger blackening the petals,
        freezing the boats in harbor;
        cruel, cunning, haywire, weeping, full astray
        in the Gehenna of anger, O in mercy, take it away.
        Having filled my mouth with dust, the Serpent
        lashing its tail in the desert of its victories.

Mercy on me Spirit,
        for pursuing my own wild will, which will not cease
        whether mercy be delivered or withheld.
        I think you told me this as you told
        the dolphin *leap*, as you told the red bear *roar*.
        Mercy for such hatred aimed at heaven, for such tongue
        that between blessing and blasphemy made a note
        sometimes of silver. For my breast of sorrows,
        for my breast of music: indivisible.
        I have fought Thee till my will be done.
        I have said to the mountain, *Be lifted*
        from your place and hurled into the sea!
        and so stand here waiting. Mercy I ask
        between dark and morning, suddenly so high, so lifted up;
        mercy I ask for one little dance, this one more,
        transfigured with forgetting.

A CHRISTMAS POEM

Maybe they shouldn't have asked for a Christmas poem from me,
unless what they wanted was some ditty, knowing and ironic,
on the theme of "disappointment," or some discourse on the
unbridgeable gulf between reality and desire. My mother's creche
is in some box in the closet, under some other box with all the
streamers and bulbs and precious baby animals which hung
upon I've lost count now of how many trees.
I swear to God, somewhere in tissue is the first candy cane
my chubby baby fingers hung on a low-hanging branch,
saved and preserved, I suppose, against the awful
mutability of the world, shattered, inedible, hardened, embittered
wherever it was soft and sweet before, held together
by packaging, exactly like the rest of us.

I don't put a tree up anymore.
I say it's because of the cats, because I travel so much.
It's really because I sit in the twinkling light of it and sob,
and I don't know why.

If you want THAT kind of poem, I'm your man. Believe me,
I know what people mean when they say that Christmas is
the worst time of year, what with the stores playing fifteen carols
we hate for every one we kind of can endure, what with
plastic poinsettias in aisles at Halloween and the churches
hoping for a windfall from parishioners who come with
liquid checkbook and guilty heart on Christmas Eve,
baby Jesus freezing on the porch amid the unresponsive animals,
the likes of us going about with hands jammed in our pockets
and eyes glued down against the panhandlers and well wishers
whom we would with equal fervor
strike from our sight above the dirty snow.

If that's what you want to hear, all right.

Or that the guns of war have not ceased tonight, and will not,
Prince of Peace or no.
The Little Match Girl will die in the cold and Tiny Tim
will be blocked by his HMO from getting the operation.

When I set up a creche of my own someday,
the Child will have as his attendants rhino and buffalo
whuffing in the stalls, the rafters heavy with tiger and panther,
their lantern eyes bright in the firelight.
The time is done
when shepherds could come out of the fields
and leave their sheep alone even for an hour.
Whatever is encamped in the nearby hills
you don't want to know about.
Sirens wail. Sad boys stand guard with rifles loaded.

I'll remember Herod's children tonight,
the Innocents that the world was not content
to slaughter only once.
I'll remember Matthew Shepard crucified
under the plate-sized western stars.
I'll remember the armed children with their sorrows,
boys and girls led astray to a country from which
there is no road back.
I'll remember wild souls, bewildered, raging in the broken streets,
to whom no moderating angel came.
I'll remember those sleeping their Christmas sleep,
inches from where shadows cross at midnight,
white teeth, white blades glittering.
I'll aim my song at those battalions in the middle of the air,
the choiring angels who seem so silly at a time like this,
their good news quaint with many thoughtless repetitions,
their hosannas so far off
we no longer remember how terrible they were,
their listeners, as the text says, sore afraid: those beings
blazing in the midnight air, wings unfurled
like hawks above the plain,
covering as the falcon covers, sharp, mysterious.

I'll stand tonight on the front lawn. I will whisper, O,
Come again. Come Down. Hover and cry out. Come to me.
I promise to be sore afraid.
I promise to drop whatever I am doing and find the star you mean,
and follow it. Will leave the lights on.
Will leave the doors unlocked.

I SLEEP, BUT MY HEART KEEPS VIGIL

I confuse my name with the name of God in seven languages.
This is a commentary, believe me, not of arrogance,
but of horror:
the oiled beard, the nimbus of spears,
the laughter compelling but not infectious,
the perpetual interplay of insistence and refusal.
Animals cringe in the underbrush,
smelling a divinity, unsure whether I am
the one who slaughters or the one who protects.

I sleep, but my heart keeps vigil

Time accustoms one to a mythic context.
Cartwheel stars trouble my sleep. In the back yard,
Tyrannosaur's blood boils in the sparrow's throat.
It is possible to have learned too much.
Out of the buried cities I hoist bones mid-air.
Skulls take flesh, mouths lip,
throats again in swan's curve upward:
lemans of Uruk.
paramours of Troy and Memphis,
char-bones Juliet from the Cave of Beasts,
up, I whisper, *tell me all.*

The virgins let the lamps go out, lift their snowy hems too late.
The bridegroom wears the face a child makes retching.
The abbess lifts her bloomers for the Bolshevik.
The last saint says, *Lord, if I had heaven I would cast You down.*
The bedside pear tree whispers,
Child, you are taking this too hard.

I sleep, but my heart keeps vigil

I take it as a sign, your coming by night,
without a body, without a voice for accusation,
me mewling in the darkness as I always did,

I wake to the song of a brown bird
hidden in the rose-of-Sharon canes.
He pipes his seven notes, the last dropped down
like Figaro singing to the butterfly.
I seek him through the window, closing on my own face--
its eyes aged with inconclusive tears--
like a prisoner stumbling from Plato's cavern,
dazzled and idiotic, hopeless to make a life
among real fires and stones.

I sleep, but my heart keeps vigil

It was otherwise at first. There was the body that came
by the risen moon and again before morning–
whether it was yours no longer matters–
and the angel of our right hands was a Rose
and the angel of our breath was Myrrh
and the angel of our brawn was Oak of the Wild Wind
and the world lay in the compass of our arms
and the flower that was our two souls melded bloomed
blood-purple, bruised to perfume, white flame at the heart.
Overcome.
Overshadowed, as the Ghost poured mayhem into Mary's womb.
Undone.

When I go looking it's for your body
and your body's shadow,
for the atoms gleanable from empty air:
a weightlifter with the planet balanced
on his solid gold trapezius, a god emerging in black leather,
thunderer, gold vaulter-of-the-spheres,

black swan singing in a man's voice,
Lear in tempest, saint king with snowbanks smoking in his wake,
Christ-caught-ember barefoot in an iron garden,
one to enfold me as the chorus swells—
those viols out of empty air!--
a perfume not from any flower,
a Titan born in Hollywood
and gone by morning with the coffee made.

I think of those children, the Holy Innocents,
murdered for you in your first hours.
You grew accustomed to that sort of thing.
I offered—need I say it?—less.
As though we were types in an old rude play,
I offered the imperfect suitor, the interrupted bridegroom,
shaggy and stinking, heart's blood cupped
in the hollow of the throat.
I offered Pierrot hesitant beyond the garden wall,
hearing the music but not daring to enter,
dancing my little dance beneath the moon.

I sleep, but my heart keeps vigil

Sometimes I think that, river-like, my occupation's
taking leave. How many nights, tormentor-spirit,
would I have taken leave of Thee, would I have thrown
the fatal mistletoe, would I have prodded the black boar
from the underbrush to see you borne still on a litter
of savory and steel, the widows keening and the
virgins wringing their dark hair? But ever by the end
I am in the vision, too, wailing *ochone* with the others
with the red torch guttering in my hand, crying you to
jump back shouting as you always have.
Love's blood turns, of course, to flowers,
autumnal flowers, snow-white for the coming white,
smoke-purple for the bier on which we thought you burned,
blood red, blood-purple at the heart.

I call at the resurrected Dancer at the center of the lights,
Love, love, remember me, who neither hears nor turns.
Peace; I will not let this bad time judge

My need tonight is violent and absolute.
The landscape calls for lions, for hyenas
loping one last foray before dawn, eyes aflame,
the bear-sized horrors of the Pleistocene.
Birds hunch dazed in the branches. I could touch them
in their stupor before the first dawn song.
The city is a red prisoner bound by mountains.
Among men only the guilty are awake,
unrighteous spirits shackled to their reveries,
invisible on their rounds, or nearly,
naming the things of the quiet world to themselves
as a father watches in sleep a child
too wild to nestle in his arms.

I'm not without comforters. I acknowledge that.
The blue lizard upheld me.
The plaint of the screech owl in the darkened trees.
The natter of the she-wrens in the hour of owls.
The bare chest dancers under the arches by the river,
the kissing of throats, ribs, eyelids in the time
when names were forgotten under the warrior moon,
the gold that lay on the rooftops when I woke
enfolded in a haze of cloud of musk
and gold shot silk. Upheld,
I say, as if accidentally, by these hundred moments
spread over the ten thousand days, unlooked-for,
irretrievable, sweet, lost, spare and sweet. All but enough.

I confuse your name with the name of gods
who for my music will forgive me everything.

  I sleep, but my heart keeps vigil,

the clock on the night stand ticking,
the monsters gathered in the hall,
the panther and the she-wolf,
the saber-tooth unfolding in the rose bush,
the drowning rivers singing in the garden.
I begin the tale again, like some mother
with her sick child beside her needing sleep,
telling of the angel who was my right hand
and the angel who was a gate of fire
all writ around with *Enter*.

Or like some idiot naming one thing over and over,
heart's wound, blood rose, hurt hawk,
black swan holding the white swan to the moon,
failed friend, fouled tabernacle, flame-gone-out
and haunting from the far hill,
inconstancy, betrayal, exhaustion, and denial

who alone is loved forever

I sleep, but my heart keeps vigil.

WHERE CAIN'S WIFE CAME FROM

There must have been something before Cain.
There must have been invention and discovery,
wars, kings, sorrows, but so strong was his coming
that nobody remembered "before"
except in shadows and rumors,
so strange was his hammering on the doors
of our fragile huts with blood on him
and the howl of an animal inside.

There must have been a home before the world,
for he said that from the first we have been
lost here, and afraid,
like people wandering dream-like
far from an unremembered home.
I hadn't thought of it before,
but he is right.
Were this our country we would know
the Voice calling in thunder on the mountains
and the will of the river flowing southward
into strange stars.

We must have dwelt for generations
on banks of streams feeding that
vast south-running god, the brown one
beautiful and deadly. We ate fish
and waterfowl and what the boldest of us
stole from the forest itself, the forest
more terrible than the river, where lay
silence in ambush and darkness stalking,
beast-haunted, the hunters, tramplers,
coilers, snappers, rippers, lurkers, who
cannot be taken but by great stealth or great luck.
We slept behind fires and palings, and mud walls
covered with watchman. We huddled on a blade of shore
wedged between the forest and the flood.

Cain when he came was hot with fury.
I have warred on God, he cried.
"What god?" I asked him. "River?"
It was not the river.
Moon-face or star-face? It was not them.
Lion or Serpent or the Thunder Mountain?
Not them, but when I said, "Mountain,"
Cain looked westward to the blue ridge of them.
He'd come that way. Like a baby he cried.
I bound his feet in white cloth where the ridges
tore them. I asked again, "What god?"
The Lord our God He is one, Cain said,
opening his arms into the room.
My people made Cain holy among us,
for he had seen a god,
and that god weeping and lamenting before him,
the mark of god across him like a tiger's stripe.

I loved him and he stayed with me.

He could make the land grow what he wanted.
It was easier for us than before.
He dried fruit to make it last
through times when fruit had vanished from the trees.
He wouldn't hunt in the forest or raise a weapon at all.
He was not afraid. The other men saw
what he brought us, and let him be.
Always at first of morning and last of dusk
he looked westward to the mountains
that mark the world's end.
He told me tales his mother told him
of the land still farther west where grew
a garden, and never any fear from the beasts there,
but she rode the lion's back
and drank beside skittery antelope.

I thought he must be child of two gods.
He said no, but his father slept
in the arms of God, and his father's grief
was god's grief always.

So a man came to us with a god's flail at his back.
I listened when he told
how the honey-guide leads to the hive,
how a damp fire smokes the bees to sleep;
how to remember that the rains come ever
at the same circuit of the stars.
When night points to rain,
we listen for the river
to come up and wander in the huts.
He taught me to whisper to the dark where God is.
He taught me the planting and the gathering up.
My people loved him. I was happy.

One dry season, though I had not swollen,
I knew the child was in me.
He wanted the child born in his father's house,
and I wished to see the land beyond the mountains,
so we gathered our things and left my home.
The journey was long. High up, newborn rivers
gush from rivers stiff white like a field of flowers.
We saw the storms that would swell my people's river.
I was glad to descend at last on the west.
I was big then and went slowly.
We set foot on a golden plain. It was Cain's land,
and he leapt in his step. We came upon a woman
tilling, even as he had taught us.
She ran to us calling, "Daughter! Son!" All was as he said.
His mother became my mother, and we lived in peace.
Her sons and mine grew strong around us.
When they were born, Father Adam
lifted them to the sky and said their names for God to hear,
the birth-blood trickling to his elbows.

They slept in the cradle of his hands.

Cain kept the strangeness in him,
the mark across him like a tiger's stripe.
If I touched it in his sleep he would cry out.
One morning when the harvest was in, I woke
to find him gone. I did not cry until I saw
his footprints in the fine dust of the doorway.
My family was about me, and there was much to do.
I reach for him at night, forgetting.
Years flew. Eve's sons and mine went to
garner wives among my people. They continued
east or south and word no longer came to us.
Father Adam lay down one day, and we buried him.
Then we women stood alone.

Eve said, "Let us go wandering like the men."
I knew where.
I knew her heart leaned westward where she
came into the world, that garden.
We made ready, wrapped dates and bread in our shawls,
laughing like girls. I did not look back
when I left my father's huts by the river,
I did not look back at Adam's plain. Eve did.
I went ahead, pretending to trample a path for her.
I was happy walking by day and resting by night.
I saw why men do this, the freedom.
Weeks we walked. Rain would blacken our fields
and my sisters would be listening for the waters.
Mother Eve said little, but she was happy.
We called ourselves girls and liked having our way.

At last the weather dried and there were strange birds
and I feared for water.
But Eve said it was close, and we went on.
Neither the coughing of the lions at night
not the day-heat stopped her. We tramped
by sun and star and I was very tired.

At last we came to a great river, and on the far side
a desert of cinders, red, barren.
Eve stared across the water for a long time.
She wept, calling the name of the garden, calling Adam.
Then she fell silent. I asked if she wanted
a fording place, but she shook her head.
We sat. She told me to go back,
but I waited, staring with her over the river
so there would be one to bury her. When it was finished,
I raised a cairn over her and went south

to seek my own.

JULIAN

Witch the lakemen call her, this wind
switching northwest with Pole ice
bunched at her tits, whipping the barges
    into harbor, beaching everything not anchored down.
    Only ladies are left, leave last.
The princess falls among the dragons.
The mantis snags a blown leaf with her
    saw-tooth arms, bites the pointless gold,
    swiveling her green head toward starvation.
Sisters beat southward from the Great Slave,
their gray harp wings in the moonlight.
    There is not enough to fight for.

    We are not in our right minds.
Dreams hurry day down with a prod of stars.
Heart flaps in dawn wind crying *betrayed*
    It is not as we were promised in the sleep
    that cradled us between the worlds,
not as the bird that matined us.
Not the Garden whose plush these feet were made for.
    Madness rides the witch's broomstick.
    Madness for armor, madness for wings,
cross, crown, chrism;
madness of endurance: rock, root,
    gills waving in blackness, the sleepers under sleet,

    blind fear burrowing from the cold;
madness of vengeance: ice lured into light,
traitor algae greening, gathering;
    seed bound in black jackets, waiting
    to spray like flak into the wind's face,
skew blast with a baffle of leaves;
madness night-locked, straightened,
    madness to hammer through:
    Lear in storm, saint kings
with snowbanks smoking in their wakes;
Christ-caught-ember
    dancing barefoot in an iron garden.

Here is a vision shown by the strangeness of God
to a devout woman, and her name is Julian,
a recluse of Norwich, and still alive,
    who desires with her sisters by grace three gifts.
    The first is recollection,
for it was otherwise at first.
For there were angels of the morning and the evening,
    and there stood my soul in loveliness
    and the angel of my right hand was rose
and the angel of my breath was frankincense
and the angel of my brawn was oak
    and the only world was garden

and the angel of that garden was a flower.
    In the flower slept a jewel,
    and I, Julian, recluse of Norwich,
with my heart shattered it.
From its fragments
    flew three Lovers, behind them in payment
    the beast-headed-six-winged Shadow
who set the angel of my words afire.
He sits astride the bright wheel,
    breaks my body in a rain of spice.
    My hair is wet with God's tears,
bone of God's cheek bruised by bone of my belly.

For my second present, sickness.
    Sickness He gave me.
    I will not let this bad time judge.
The third, three wounds.
Wolf howled at my window.

    On his neck, a white silk knotted.
    A bright man came from nowhere
offering one stark snow lily.
Three wounds he gave me.
    He found where I had fallen in the fallen leaves,
    lifted, sang to me,

Julian. Julian.

THE HIDDEN VERSES OF IBN DAWUD
AD 909

In the Garden of Unearned Delight

There is a book in which there is no doubt,
a guide to those who seek the Way,
a comfort to those who trust in the Unseen,
who maintain the prayer
and spend only what was provided for them.
Who are certain of the Hereafter.

   This is not that book.

I sat me down in the garden
to compose the Book of Doubts.
I took a chair under the cedar trees
to compose the Song of Crossroads
where there is always a choice and never a sign.
I begin, of course, with the recitation of lineage:

Adam who heard his Father's word
and, as any son would, shrugged it off;
Abraham who, in the presence of the delectable slave girls,
       would not wait;
Moses who struck the rock twice to be sure;
our mothers and fathers, who by an hour's vanity,
a punishment unjustified, wrecked conviction
of the great Dome solid from the base to crown.

One's colleagues are righteous in the marketplace,
but when alone with their devils
they light their little candles, the needless,

the manifold, in confusion each
contradicting the others' light. What they know of God
is rolling darkness edged with lightening,
like a storm out of the desert.

   They are caught up.

The foxes hear their cries.
They will not come back.
God besieges the faithless.
Yet here I sit in the garden of unearned delights.
A catbird bathes in the still pools.
I presume He has not found me out,
the One who punishes and sets right.
I could wait a while longer.
I could set out cakes and cooling beverages—
the kind that draws the kindred I desire—
I could purify myself with limpid waters.

The catbird at the basin's rim pauses,
plucks at two feathers under his gray wing.
"Look," he says, "a dark wind whirling from the desert.
Edged with fire. "

The High Places of Babylon

The high places of Babylon sink like ships into the sand.
Jackals haunt the temple precincts.
Owl vomits spent mice upon the implements of queens.
The River lifted her skirts and went another way.
It's all in the Hebrew prophets,
what comes of too much victory,
of taste exceeding in refinement, apparently, God's own.

Yet I pick my way to the dead city
with a blue hood over my head.

Bring a tidbit for the jackals and they'll let you pass.
I find comfort here. I find comfort
walking in the world that was before the world began,
before the Instruction, before the stern Instructor
at once imperative and ambiguous.

I come here for heart's ease, for the blood
and purple flowers brought from the world's end
a thousand years ago and set in a garden that is gone,

themselves enduring, miraculous, for this little while.
The Scriptures name a thousand ways to die.
A broken heart is not among them. Yet that is the portal
open before me. One chooses less than is supposed.

I say to the high places of Babylon,
"Be revealed in all the wicked glory that once was!"
Owl answers, the jackal bitch with the
shadows of her little ones lined up behind her
in the moonlight. This is what comes of everything.
It is an unexpected comfort. I might die of what I please.
I might curl up in the sands and be forgotten.
The lights of living Baghdad glitter in the distance.
When it is dust, lovers shall come to the ruined places,
to the jackal haunted precincts, the gore-stained tiles
and the twisted stems, to the empery of owls.
Someone will have told them that someone, sometime
died for love. They will wait under the traversing moon
until they hear a voice, not knowing any longer it is mine.

The Conversation between Ibn Jami, Ibn Dawud

1

I will put a veil over my face before I go into the street.
I will place a veil because in the mirror I saw such beauty.
I want nobody to see it before you.

Through the shadowed streets and the sunstruck ones
people will be wondering, "What could lie behind the veil?
Some great beauty hoarded for a lover,
or sad disfigurement hidden from mockers and pityers."
Only you will know, when I am safely gathered
in the walled garden, when the nightingales have ceased
their calling in the hour of first light.
I will hear your footsteps approach across the tiles.
I will await . When you say, "What?" I'll lift the veil.
You will cry out, "God is great!." Of all the Faithful
crying that in the vaulted mosques at first prayer call,
you alone know what it means.

2

My love awaited in the garden as the day broke.
He wore a veil in honor of the veil the world
wears at that hour, covering the scarlet and the ivory,
covering the black curve of brows like the moon
of a backwards universe bowed in its white night.

I don't know what he expected when he raised the veil.
I fell down onto the little flowers, knees wet with dew,
crying, "God is great!" Only the Faithful
in the vaulted mosque knew what I meant.
Lovers overheard me crying the words into God's breast.

3

I see my father striding in from the desert,
leaning on his staff of wild thorn.
His one robe, his one wife, the one road
received from the Prophet from which he never varied.
I meet him at the gate, so he will not be mocked
for his simplicity–as I in fact mock him,
the creases on his face reddened with dust,
the difficult language he speaks
in which there is only yes and no.

"I have a beloved," I say. He smiles,
for this is "yes" and it is grandchildren
and it is him at the font of a flood of progeny.
I tell him the beauty of my beloved is the swift
sun on the face of the Two Rivers, gold and
ravishing, hemmed about with the long-legged birds.
I tell him I veil my face to let my eye light on nothing
before the face of my beloved rising soft from sleep.
He knows I am a poet.

I regale him with verses learned
in the Caliph's waiting room.
I feed him with delicacies he had not dreamed of.
I bathe his body in the scented oils.
Laden him with gifts for the journey home.

He says, "Son, it is time to speak the truth." I say,
The truth is this: against your advice
I have come to the labyrinth and was not lost.
I have come to the garden of deceptions
and was not deceived."

4

The difficult poetry of the mystics maintains
that God's second witness are those damned for love,
whose hellfire is the fire of love
from which they would not be released.
Their flower is the rose, betrayed by its own intricacies.
Their flower is narcissus, who gazes
at one still point forever.
Their element is flame that rekindles desire anew
even as desire is by many violences attained.

Even the damned are lovers, whose ways
are longer than the world, the dark rose and the dark road
they are treading until the unforeseeable coming home,
when God Himself cries "Ah!" We are blessed

in a God who suffers Himself to be loved.
We are blessed in the God who sows Himself
among the bodies that all love might be His.
I have awakened from dreams in which God is my lover
into the room where you are my lover and perceived

no time has passed, no space traversed--
lips to His lips, heart to His heart in yours.
I know you are coming veiled to me through dark streets,
that when you arrive I will cry out "Who?"
and when the veil is raised I will not know you.
I will fall upon my knees crying the Holy Names
one must not cry but at that hour
I know that my heart's blood will stream upon the tiles.
That you will bend. That you will lift me up.

THE SAINT FRANCIS POEMS

I

Bernard of Quintavalle to His Lady Poverty

To my poor mother, and her poor mother
before her yet more poor, and hers,
most excellent in want, and to all
who lacked before us I pray now
for the gift of graceful hungering,
to have dearth as a rich man's table meats,
    to dwell in penury abundant.

I say to my companions, look over winter.
Hazel shrub is more miserable than we:
fruitless, leafless, naked to the snow.
Dare we break her poor self
for fire to warm us?
"Yes," they answer, unmoved. Too rich yet.
    I say to them, "rather let us

take off our coats, invite gale against us.
Let us peel our shirts to lie down
with the rocks and sleet.
Give such glory to the flesh
as to wear our little skins for fire and roof."
This Saint Hazel taught us.
    This we hoard for riches.

I ask my companions dare we
pitch camp in sight of a rich man's house?
"Yes," they answer, "having come so far."
Come then, I tell them, farther.
This is the man who feeds his beggars
lessons and fills the empty cup
    with exhortation.

This is the man who cannot kneel
around his belly and who prays
to the Virgin with breakfast on his breath.
Light through his windows on the snow
falls rose and jonquil.
We will not rest here. Holily
we eat our hunger, drink the frozen road.

I say to my companions, "we are not poor enough."
An old owl bears less,
ascends more near to heaven.
Too rich.
Were hell a river we would drop.
Were heaven an island in a stream, we'd sink
    and leave our fine hats floating.

I tell my companions we have no song
plain, no cold shank bare,
no prospect bleak enough.
Rich men tempt and gift us,
thinking there must be some trick.
Give them all that they can carry.
When our eyes stare out with famine

they'll decide they want no more.
As they puff laden down the road,
think of bridges only light and bird pass over.
We must go that way.
We are rich yet.
On the day we wake and think ourselves alone,
    we shall be almost poor enough.

O Lady Poverty, I am fat among your swains.
I sing to you as soft-eyed men
to their loves all sweetly on a summer day.

If I cannot be the briar, I shall be the rose.
If no beggar, then the lord of worlds.
If not the very desert,
    then some paradise a fool

might wander in and think God made.
I say to my companions,
"keep nothing but desire,"
So she who worlds and fountains in desire
might welcome us, bare as any hazel
she would dress with white,
light as a bird to whom her hands are open.

II

Leo, Brother Little Lamb of God, to Lady Chastity

Now, my friends, far to the south
and inland is a mount
that smokes from its streams at morning.
All upon that mountain grow the trees,
and in the shadow of the trees
blooms one blood-red rhododendron.
 None has seen it. None touched.

Under the blood-red rhododendron
in the witching of the million trees,
a milk snake loops his magic circle.
No color is lacking from his scale
by slanted light. Think of his
against our Lady's glory, scale
against hair that, blowing in silence,

sets the first of day aflame.
I woke and saw a girl swell
in the bark of trees. I saw summer
turn womanly down into the valley
with high breasts and a thousand arms of flowers.
I reached to touch;
 flesh undid the dream.

The village wife come to fill her pail
sends her hair behind as rain
sends musks of forests.
 I do not know whether this requires of me

homage or judgment. Christ forgive;
I stand and drink as one drinks
thunder from the sea.

To what love shall I sing?
I have nothing but love, love abundant,
love unspent, untarnished, rising wave-like
till the sea is drowned.
Who would love me like this back again?
Love is all I keep, the word unsaid,
the hand withdrawn that the heart might seize.

Once our master watched me watching.
He said, "Leo, come in and say
what a woman's walk has told you.
If it is wrong, we are too small to know."
So I spoke of a Lady who is love,
who for my fidelities
        is lost to me forever.

My Lady Wanting, without you is no lover.
Without you is but taking and the need again.
If a woman cut her hair in quiet,
let the strands blow across the grass
for the moles, the nests of birds,

I'd love her then for what she could not give.
        Lutenists have touched their throats
for music in a woman's praise until
I have no taste for any further sweetness.
But for another savor,
bitter and beautiful.
If she fell darkened of her eyes,
bereft of all the silver stirring,
  shadow then in shadow, black

but for her break in black space,
I would love, as love is empty.
I would as the gardener loves
the singing west that is the rain,
as the soldier loves the enemy who
bleeds beside him on the lost field.

I would love, Queen Chasteness, as a man

loves what fades by morning from his clenched hand.
Day comes to light the space in my heart.
She enters then, this Lady,
careful that I look away.
I wait; who's loved in emptiness
is loved forever.
     Lady, rain your hair around me.

III

Clara Scifi Consults the Flowering Crab Concerning Her Lord
Obedience

I have been obedient two or three days together.
I danced for the one-eyed fiddler man,
gave bread to the rich to make them wonder.
I held a cardinal rose between my teeth
to see them blush, the grave young men,
too young
  to blunt their hearts on God.

I have done sometimes what must be done.
I kissed lepers on their aching mouths.
I lay in bed a whole day
and made my sisters bring me
trays of apricots and yellow cream.
I heeded you, my savants,
 sustaining bones, wise feet, lungs

ever simple in the sea of air,
hands, nerves, attentive blood
flowing through, finding where I hunger.
I learned your ways and followed,
so to keep this world,
this hurly-burly beauty,
 this beast hock-deep in stars alive.

A ragged man knocked at my father's door.
Not the first nor the second time
that he said **follow me** did I understand
it was no request.
Thereafter I have ridden my bare feet
through briars and my rough smock
through doorways where my friends

remember me in miniver and vair.
My ragged saint said, Grieve, Clara.
The world does not remember you.
So in obedience I grieved till I grew merry in it,
and when he said rejoice , I did not know how.
I built jubilation from the ground up.
 I made my soul a body dancing over mirrors.

I have been obedient two or three days together.
I have stood looking out to sea
as though the Lord my Lover would return
beneath a billowing sail.
I've stepped into thieves' firelight, and begged,
and they gave, fearing to come
  between me and my furious acquiescence.

I've perplexed the dying with a joke,
because the time was commanded
to be glad in.
Always I have walked beside sir ragged bones
waiting if he said **rise up**
to rise, and if **lie down** to lie on straw
 and dream of satins where I lay before.

I have been obedient but for the day
I crept cat-like back into my father's garden
where the flowering crabtree wore her Whitsun,
all scarlet in the sky-blue town.
Through my rags and boils
she knew me.
  As when I was a child I curled

my hurts against her. Then I heard
the crabtree say, *Abide. Abide.*
I've kept my flowers for you an extra day.
Take the dry spear out of your side.
Pack the prickly crown away.
Sit in my shade and think your thought
of what are the goods and what's the price,

of who has loved you and who cannot,
of bony saints mewling in paradise.
I am pink in the sad gray town.
I am fire in a field of ice. Why'd
storm kiss me when it blew the steeples down?
I shake out my beautiful hair and go
   round her and round her, and do not know.

VERONICA

A unicorn tapestry,
a Cluny-work of colors set precisely
for the random falling of a snow white hoof,
the field rolls into hill and sky.
Proud grass upstarts,
greened by night rain, sizzling with clear juices.
Yellow of the lion's-tooth. White of daisy,
cornflower, the sun's eyes spying out the meadow.
White of robin-plantain,
touched with tint as though
the shadow of a cardinal star.
The pale blue is veronica, the humus-hugging speedwell.
Not whole blue, blue cloud passing over,
blue-white, the sea in a billion generations
age-bleached, roaring in broken trumpet.
The blue of heaven or a carved stone.
Close up, they're seen to radiate
a blueness outward from the heart.
Remember the legends of the flowers. If
you know a happy one, you know more than I.
This Veronica's blossom bears the imprint of a face,
a corona stained by sweat or blood upon a white veil.
Blue of the wounds tricks the eye to whiteness.
The patch of speedwell
troubles the field as though
a cloth were dropped by someone hurrying.
The mowers hold off.
Old wives say,

Veronica cleanseth the blood of all corruption.

Whether or not, it cures the wasted places.
 Scorning trample and trash, it wins whole fields.
    Like its sorrowing namesake
    at the Passover roadside, it does not
      note our engagement in the intricacies of passion,
      if we deny, cry out, or proceed some duller way.

A PASSION PLAY

Easter rises from the plain of days
like Binns Crest from its skirt of cows.
Here are the low hills that have stared
into our windows like a mad uncle
since the first thing we remember.
Here is our perfectable little town,
our historic Main Street, our Founder's Elm
saved from blight at great expense.
Here is Kiwanis Park with its green benches,
its white wedding cake gazebo.
This is the make-shift stage
sweet with sawn wood.
This is the Passion Play.
The bleachers are full, not merely with our own,
but with folks from Lisbon and across the river,
in the lot a license plate from Indiana.
Same story always, but the players change.
Now behind the rope-and-blanket curtain,
high school track coach Lord Christ
ties his blond hair back with Nazarene simplicity.
The Queen of Heaven folds her apron for a day,
counting not the lost tips, but bearing witness
by breast-curve, by leap of thighs
to God among the bleachers.
Magdalene's children gawk from the shade
of the Cola sign, their mother changed before them,
her cloud hair floating on the wind.

I wondered what I'd be this year.
Not fierce Christ in these merchant's bones,
surely, nor the man-storm Peter,
not Herod, Caiphas, the villains
whose dedication astonishes even the saints.
Not Judas, sympathetic in the modern way,
by mad Israel tormented,
by the dawdling Incarnation
driven to desperate acts.
As I child I was the last, mute angel.
I hoped at best for the Centurion Who Believed,

the sleepy guard pillowed on Christ's coat,
Nicodemus who is troubled at night
and goes dangerously to see the Master,
who thinks God might raise a prophet if He please,
even from the midden of Galilee.

But they said, *You, John.*
The beginning was that word.
After a few rehearsals in my dusty robe,
a few splinters through my sandals
I became Christ's beloved,
who in the paintings leans in closest.
It was glory walking with him.
Pharisees bent to their books, rebuked.
Rich men snipped the bangles from their clothes.
I danced a little in my walk
to walk so with a god who loved me.

Then there was nothing but raw crossed wood,
a wrecked man willing me a mother,
all crushed and weeping worse than in the script.
Our voices skittered down the grass
like flushed birds, tinny, husky, gone.
The crowd behind me holds its breath.
I want to turn to them
from this intolerable tableau
and say *children.*

My story comes after this.
John, Apostle, Saint John Gospel-Maker,
Eagle of the Most High, John of the Apocalypse
weeps here on a wooden plank, my Lord
bleeding between two sticks,
the Holy City yet unseen,
floating bright Jerusalem mothering her beasts
and angels in the Lamb's white fleece forever,
flame, a gulf of fire, a city on Binns Crest
templed with the sun and moon.

Three minutes on the stage means three days.
East of us, a light.
This is poor John at the empty tomb.
I know what is coming.
I grip my beard in my two hands and laugh.
I must run to tell the others.

I WILL TELL YOU WHEN I REACH THE END

1

Before morning,
following the twisty stone path.
Only the moon allows this,
getting to each stone before me,
waiting till I am solid,
leaping to the next before I do.

2

Oh, there is the lumpy road and there
the strange light in the neighbors' yard.
You make for them. You return
into the embrace of everything you know.
Stepping lightly, stepping heavy—
a witness will know better than yourself.

3

The twisty path of stone I take by moonlight
always leads the same place.
I think it might not, once.
I took it this morn before morning
thinking it might not lead where it led.
Who knows? I will tell you when I reach the end.

SOME DAY, IN THE EMERGENCE
FROM THIS FIERCE INSIGHT,
LET ME SING JUBILATION AND
PRAISE TO ASSENTING ANGELS.

RAINER MARIA RILKE
DUINO ELEGIES
THE TENTH ELEGY

TRANSLATE BY A.S. KLINE © 2001

ACKNOWLEDGMENTS

The Annunciation, Carol of the Christ Child's Garden, Carol
of the Infuriated Hour:
  Image
Christmas Morning: *Stone Country*
"Gazelle Drinking from One of the Rivers of Paradise":
  Epoch
The Hidden Verses of Ibn Dawud, Hymn to the Blessed
Virgin Mary,
I Will Tell You when I Reach the End:
  Harbinger Asylum
Julian, Sassetta: the Meeting of St. Anthony and St. Paul,
Where the Wife of Cain Came from:
  The Third Wind
On the Adoration of the Shepherd, On the Vigil of Saint
Thomas:
  Windhover
A Passion Play: *Mid-American Review*
The Saint Francis Poems: *The Literary Review*,
Veronica: *The Nebraska Review*
Who Is That Walking in My Garden: *One*

ABOUT THE AUTHOR

David Brendan Hopes was born in Akron, Ohio, and has lived in Asheville, North Carolina–where he is Professor of English at UNCA– since 1983. In addition to being a poet, he is a fiction and non-fiction writer, a painter, an actor, and a widely produced playwright. *PENIEL* is his fourth full-length collection of poetry.

www.ingramcontent.com/pod-product-compliance
Lightning Source LLC
LaVergne TN
LVHW091313080426
835510LV00007B/480